Correlation in Credit Risk

Xiaoling Pu
Xinlei Zhao

Office of the Comptroller of the Currency

OCC Economics Working Paper 2009-5

Version Date: February 2, 2010

Keywords: Correlations, credit risk, credit spread, macroeconomic conditions, industry effect.
JEL Classifications: G28, G33.

Xiaoling Pu is an Assistant Professor in the Department of Finance, Kent State University; Xinlei Zhao is a Financial Economist in the Credit Risk Analysis Division at the Office of the Comptroller of the Currency and an Associate Professor in the Department of Finance, Kent State University. Please address correspondence to Xinlei Zhao, Office of the Comptroller of the Currency, 250 E St. SW, Washington, DC 20219 (phone: 202-927-9960; e-mail: xinlei.zhao@occ.treas.gov).

The views expressed in this paper are those of the authors alone and do not necessarily reflect those of the Office of the Comptroller of the Currency or the U.S. Department of the Treasury. The authors would like to thank Min Qi, Paul Dawson, and participants of the 2009 Asian Financial Management Association meeting and research seminars at Kent State University and the Office of the Comptroller of the Currency for their insightful comments and editorial assistance. The authors take responsibility for any errors.

Correlation in Credit Risk

Xiaoling Pu
Xinlei Zhao

February 2010

Abstract: We examine the correlation in credit risk using credit default swap (CDS) data. We find that the observable risk factors at the firm, industry, and market levels and the macroeconomic variables cannot fully explain the correlation in CDS spread changes, leaving at least 30 percent of the correlation unaccounted for. This finding suggests that contagion is not only statistically but also economically significant in causing correlation in credit risk. Thus, it is important to incorporate an unobservable risk factor into credit risk models in future research. We also find, consistent with some theoretical predictions, that the correlation is countercyclical and is higher among firms with low credit ratings than among firms with high credit ratings.

I. Introduction

Correlation in credit risk is a well-known phenomenon. Understanding the causes of correlated credit losses is crucial for many purposes, such as managing a portfolio, setting capital requirements for banks, and pricing structured credit products that are heavily exposed to correlations in credit risk; for example, collateralized debt obligations (CDO). This issue has become particularly important because of the rapid growth of structured credit products in the financial markets in recent years. But despite much research on the subject, we do not understand many aspects of correlation in credit risk; this paper attempts to move the literature forward.

First, we explore the economic importance of contagion in credit risk correlation. This is an open empirical question. Many credit models are based on the doubly stochastic assumption that, conditional on observable risk factors, defaults are independent of each other. This assumption is widely accepted and implemented in banking to determine capital requirements. However, the assumption has been challenged by Das and colleagues (2007), and their findings are supported by Duffie and colleagues (2008). Evidence exists that contagion has a notable impact on the correlation in credit risk of firms subject to significant credit events (Jorion and Zhang 2007). On the basis of these findings, some researchers have tried to include contagion in credit models (e.g., Duffie et al. 2008, Giesecke 2004, Jarrow and Yu 2001, and Schönbucher and Schubert 2001).

However, the economic importance of contagion in a firm's credit risk correlation is not clear from the literature. If the role of contagion is statistically significant but not economically significant, modeling contagion may not be of first-order importance. But even though some researchers and practitioners reject the doubly stochastic assumption, they find that the proportion of correlation in credit risk that cannot be explained by observable risk factors is small (1 to 5 percent), which suggests that unobservable risk factors may be of minor importance in credit risk models. In this paper, we attempt to clarify this issue.

We also explore the credit risk correlation pattern over time and across firms with varying credit quality. The academic literature cannot agree on these patterns either. For example, Erlenmaier and Gersbach (2001) and Zhou (2001) suggest that the correlation should increase with default probability, whereas Das and colleagues (2006) and Lopez (2002) find the opposite. Further, Das and colleagues (2006) find that fluctuations in credit risk correlation are not countercyclical, a finding that runs counter to the theoretical predictions of Gersbach and Lipponer (2000) and Erlenmaier and Gersbach (2001).

These questions are important because credit risk has been and still is the biggest risk facing banks. And with securitization and the new products that have been developed in the financial market, credit risk has been spread out beyond the banking sector to various market segments. Ambiguity regarding these issues poses serious challenges for investors, practitioners, and regulators.

In this paper, we approach credit risk in two ways. First, unlike earlier studies, we use data from the credit default swap (CDS) market. Most researchers examine the correlation in a firm's credit risk using either estimated default intensity based on actual default observations or implied default probability derived from the Merton (1974) model. The former approach may not be reliable, because some default events are strategic decisions and, therefore, may not correspond to economic default.[1] Also, some

---

[1] A famous example is Texaco's decision in the mid-1980s to enter Chapter 11 for nonfinancial reasons.

financially distressed companies may be able to negotiate debt restructuring to avoid default or may be acquired with bankruptcy looming on the horizon, and these informal resolutions of financial distress are difficult to identify.[2, 3] The problem of reliable numbers is a serious challenge—default is a low-frequency event, and any misclassification may have a major impact on the precision of parameter estimates. Thus, the estimated default intensity might be contaminated, and this weakness could be behind some rather surprising findings in the literature. For example, some studies (e.g., Duffie et al. 2008; Duffie, Saita, and Wang 2007; and Figlewski, Frydman, and Liang 2006) show a positive relationship between default intensity and the returns on the S&P 500 stock index.

On the other hand, default probability estimated from the Merton model could be confounded by the oversimplified assumptions behind the model.

In contrast, the CDS market enables the direct measurement of credit risk by many market participants. CDS is insurance against a default by a particular company or sovereign entity (known as the reference entity). The buyer of the CDS contract makes periodic payments to the seller for the right to sell a bond issued by the reference entity for its face value if the issuer defaults. So the price of CDS contracts (or the CDS spread) is a direct measure of the credit risk of the reference entity. Because CDS spreads can be

---

[2] For example, from 1970 through 2008, Moody's database identifies 577 bankruptcy cases and 209 distressed exchange offers. By comparison, Frank and Torous (1994) find 37 bankruptcy cases and 76 distressed exchange offers during the period 1983–1988. It seems that Moody's database may have missed some distressed exchange offers, which suggests that this informal type of resolution is very difficult to identify.

[3] The strategic decision aspect of default has been documented and modeled in some theoretical models; for example, Anderson, Sundaresan, and Tychon (1996); Bergman and Callen (1991); Frank and Torous (1989, 1994); and Gertner and Scharfstein (1991).

based on a wide array of credit risk models, it is also a comprehensive measure of credit risk.[4]

The second way we approach credit risk in this paper is by investigating the observable factors and their contributions to the correlation in risk. Although previous studies have incorporated some macroeconomic factors into modeling credit risk, the impact of these variables is not consistent across studies, and some results are counterintuitive. We study the impact on credit risk of various macroeconomic variables as well as firm- and market-level variables, and we model the industry effect on the credit risk of individual firms. Although many researchers have suggested that the industry effect partially accounts for the correlation in credit risk, the literature has yet to provide conclusive evidence.

On the basis of monthly changes in CDS spreads from January 2001 through December 2006, we find that changes in CDS spreads are positively correlated, with an average correlation of 21 percent. Observable variables at the firm level can reduce the correlation by 8 percent, resulting in a correlation of 13 percent among the regression residuals. Market-level and macroeconomic variables are significantly associated with changes in CDS spreads, with the expected signs of the regression coefficients. These variables, together with firm-level variables, can reduce the correlation by two-thirds to 7 percent. We also confirm the existence of the industry effect and find that firms in less cyclical industries have lower correlations in credit risk. Although industry variables are

---

[4] However, using the CDS data also involves some potential disadvantages. One is the liquidity risk; we use the monthly data to mitigate this problem. Another problem is that CDS includes the counterparty risk (i.e., the credit risk of the sellers of the CDS contracts). However, we argue that our results should not be materially affected by the counterparty risk; we use data from before 2006, and the large financial institutions were considered to be rather safe before the financial crisis began.

significantly related to CDS spread changes in the right directions, the industry effect can be responsible for less than 1 percent of the correlation in CDS spread changes after we control for firm-level, market-level, and macroeconomic variables.

When all observable variables are combined, they can account for about 14 percent of the correlations, leaving 7 percent unaccounted for. The main observable variables that contribute to the correlations are firm-level variables and credit spreads, which can be affected by both contagion and systematic risks. Excluding these variables, the mean correlation among the residuals is 12 percent. These findings suggest that contagion could contribute from 33 percent to 57 percent of the correlation in credit risks. This magnitude is much higher than that reported by Das and colleagues (2007) and is economically significant.

We also investigate the potential nonlinearity in the relationship between credit risk and observable variables, and find that accounting for nonlinearity does not qualitatively change our findings. Thus, the evidence suggests that contagion does play an economically important role in the credit risk correlation.

In addition, we find that the correlation in credit risk is countercyclical; that is, it is higher during economic downturns and lower during booms. Also, it is higher among firms with low credit ratings than among those with high credit ratings. These findings are consistent with some theoretical predictions but not with the findings based on measures from the Merton model. We believe that the results derived from CDS spreads are more reliable because of the oversimplified assumptions behind Merton's model and the evidence in the literature that the Merton default probability measure does not forecast default probability well (see, e.g., Bharath and Shumway 2007; Jones, Mason, and Rosenfeld 1984; and Zhou 2001).

Although our study period was short, it included one full business cycle; thus, our results should have general implications. The study period did not include the recent market turmoil; however, if contagion is a major phenomenon during severe economic downturns, failing to include the recent period of turmoil is biased only against the finding that contagion plays an important role. Our evidence, therefore, suggests that modeling the unobservable risk factors should be of first-order importance for future research in credit modeling.

This paper is organized as follows. In section II, we review the current literature. In section III, we describe our sample. We discuss observable risk factors and their contributions to the correlation in credit risk in section IV. Section V presents results on the correlation in credit risk over time and by rating groups. In the last section, we draw a brief conclusion.

II. Literature Review

Modeling Correlation in Credit Risk

The two branches of credit risk measurement are (1) the structural approach and (2) the reduced-form approach. Structural models originate from the Merton (1974) model and assume that a company will default if the value of its assets is below a certain level; for example, the amount of its outstanding debt. The key to structural modeling is to capture the stochastic asset diffusion process, and default correlation between two companies is introduced by assuming that the stochastic processes followed by the assets of the two companies are correlated. Correlation in the stochastic asset diffusion processes of two firms can be caused by both observable risk factors and unobservable risk factors, such as contagion. The advantage of structural models is the flexibility in modeling correlation in credit risk; the disadvantage is the difficulty in implementing them empirically. The general theoretical predictions from this school are that credit risk correlation is higher for firms with a low credit rating than for those with a high credit rating, and that the correlation increases during economic downturns (see, e.g., Erlenmaier and Gersbach 2001, Gersbach and Lipponer 2000, and Zhou 2001).

The reduced-form models assume that a firm's default time is driven by a default intensity that varies according to changes in macroeconomic conditions (see, e.g., Duffie and Singleton 1999; Hull and White 2001; Jarrow, Lando, and Turnbull 1995; and Lando 1998). In other words, when the default intensity for company A is high, the default intensity for company B tends to be high as well, which induces a default correlation between the two companies. The reduced-form models usually assume that observable risk factors are the main drivers of firm credit risk and that, after controlling for observable factors and default intensity, defaults should be independent. This is the doubly stochastic assumption. Because of its mathematical tractability, most researchers and practitioners gravitate toward this approach; thus, the doubly stochastic assumption is behind many commonly used reduced-form models to predict default, such as the duration models and the survival time copula models.

The doubly stochastic assumption is also the key assumption behind the proprietary models. For instance, Moody's KMV Risk Advisor considers systematic factors using a three-level approach: (1) a composite market risk factor, (2) an industry

7

and country risk factor, and (3) regional factors and sector indicators. The factor loading for an individual firm for each of the factors is estimated using asset variances obtained from the option theoretical model, and the factor loadings are then used to calculate covariances for each pair of firms. In CreditMetrics, the credit transition matrix is conditioned on a credit cycle index, which shifts down when economic conditions deteriorate. The credit cycle index is obtained by regressing default rates for speculative grade bonds on the credit spread, 10-year Treasury yield, inflation rate, and growth in gross domestic product (GDP). In contrast, Credit Risk Plus incorporates cyclical factors by allowing the mean default rate to vary over the business cycle. Credit Risk Plus models find that correlation in credit risk is higher among firms with low credit ratings.

In summary, the doubly stochastic assumption plays a critical role in the vast majority of credit models used in research and practice. Das and colleagues (2007) challenge this assumption. They find that variations in the observable factors cannot fully explain the correlation in credit risk and that the doubly stochastic assumption is violated; however, the proportion of the correlation that cannot be explained by observable factors is rather small. Their conclusion may be contaminated in two ways. First, the evidence could result from the misspecification associated with the model to predict default intensity. A different model could lead to two possibilities: (1) observable factors may be sufficient to account for the correlated default risk, as argued by Lando and Nielsen (2008), or (2) the proportion not explained by observable factors could be much larger than Das and colleagues documented. Second, because default events are rare, results based on actual default observations may contain large estimation errors, especially as this model of predicting default intensity is based on the surprising and counterintuitive finding that default intensity increases along with the equity market index.

It is not clear from the literature how the correlation in credit risk varies over business cycles and across firms with different credit quality, as studies on these subjects have yielded conflicting results. This lack of clarity poses a major challenge for investors, portfolio managers, bankers, and bank regulators.

Macroeconomic Impact in Credit Risk Modeling

Some studies incorporate macroeconomic conditions into credit risk models; however, researchers have used different macroeconomic variables, and some variables that are important in one paper are found to be unimportant in another. Also, some empirical results are quite counterintuitive.

Some researchers find intuitive relations between credit risk and macroeconomic variables. For example, Collin-Dufresne, Goldstein, and Martin (2001) examine determinants of changes in credit spreads using changes in 10-year Treasury rates, changes in the slope of the yield curve, changes in market volatility, and monthly S&P 500 returns. They find that all these variables are significantly related to changes in credit spreads, with the direction implied by structural models. Carling and colleagues (2007) investigate how macroeconomic conditions affect business defaults using a corporate portfolio from a leading Swiss retail bank. They find that the output gap, the yield curve, and consumers' expectations of future economic development can help explain a firm's default risk.

Other researchers use different variables and come to different conclusions. Duffie and colleagues (2007) use three-month Treasury bill rates and the trailing one-year return on the S&P 500 index to predict default intensity. They find that default intensity is significantly negatively related to the short-term interest rate and positively related to the S&P 500 index. The latter finding is counterintuitive: default intensity should be lower in a booming market. Duffie and colleagues have also tried 10-year Treasury yields, U.S. personal income growth, GDP growth rate, AAA-BAA bond yield spread, and industry-average distance to default; they found that these variables were not significant in predicting default. Das and colleagues (2007) used the same model and found that industrial growth played only a limited role, a finding corroborated by Duffie and colleagues (2008). Similarly, Lando and Nielsen (2008) include S&P 500 returns, three-month Treasury yields, industrial production, and term spread in their prediction of default intensity. They find that default intensity is negatively related to industrial production but find no relationship between default intensity and the three-month Treasury yield. They find a positive relationship between default intensity and both S&P 500 returns and term spread, which is somewhat counterintuitive.

Couderc and Renault (2005) investigate the impact on default intensity of a number of market and macro variables. They find that default intensity is positively related to market volatility, term spread, and yield difference between BBB bonds and AAA bonds, and negatively related to market return, Treasury yield, real GDP growth rate, industrial production growth rate, inflation, personal consumption growth, and the spread of BBB bonds over Treasury bonds. Their findings on market return are intuitive, although they differ from those of Duffie and colleagues (2007) and Lando and Nielsen (2008). Their results on the term spread are different from those of Carling and colleagues (2007) and Collin-Dufresne and colleagues (2001), and the negative relationships between default intensity and both BBB spread and inflation are counterintuitive.

In summary, the impact of macroeconomic variables is not consistently documented in the literature, and some results are counterintuitive. These findings add to the puzzle of whether observable risk factors can explain the correlation in credit risk. We believe that the inconsistent and sometimes counterintuitive findings may be contaminated by the noise in the default data, as default events are rare and can contain misclassifications that lead to estimation errors. CDS data are more suitable for this purpose.

III. Data Description and Sample Statistics

The Sample

The primary data in this study are the monthly CDS data from January 2001 through December 2006. We use the five-year CDS, as this instrument is the most liquid in the CDS market (Hull, Predescu, and White 2004). We use monthly data to match the monthly macroeconomic variables because price movements in monthly data are less contaminated than daily or weekly data by temporary imbalances between supply and demand. The CDS spread measures total credit risk, which includes both default probability (DP) and losses given default (LGD). It is widely documented that DP and LGD are positively correlated (see, e.g., Gupton, Hamilton, and Berthault 2001); thus, the CDS spread is a comprehensive measure of total credit risk.

We downloaded the CDS data from Reuters, then merged them with CRSP (Center for Research in Security Prices) and quarterly Compustat data. Our sample includes 523 firms (25,113 firm-month observations)—376 investment-grade firms and 147 speculative-grade firms, based on the average rating for each firm during the sample period. We obtained ratings data from Moody's. Our sample period (2001–2006) includes one full business cycle consisting of varying economic conditions: an economic downturn in the early period, a recovery in 2003, and a normal period afterward. [5]

Variables at the Firm, Industry, and Market Levels

We use three firm-level variables to explain the changes in CDS spreads:[6] monthly stock returns,[7] monthly stock volatility change, and firm leverage change.[8] According to the structural model, a firm's default risk is higher when either volatility or leverage is high. Also, stock returns indicate the market's assessment of a firm's future performance. Lower returns imply a dimmer outlook, which should correlate with a higher credit risk, so stock returns should be negatively associated with changes in CDS spreads.

We use the following market-level variables: changes in implied market volatility (VIX), changes in market leverage, and changes in market returns (measured by NYSE-

---

[5] We included firms that experienced credit events, so our sample does not suffer from the survivorship bias.

[6] Throughout the paper, we report results on the basis of percentage changes in CDS spreads (i.e., $CDS\ Spread\ Change_{t-1} = \dfrac{CDS\ Spread_t - CDS\ Spread_{t-1}}{CDS\ Spread_{t-1}}$. Results using log changes in CDS spreads are very similar.

[7] We have tried excess stock returns rather than actual stock returns, and the results do not change qualitatively.

[8] We obtained monthly stock returns from the CRSP database. We estimated monthly stock volatility from daily stock returns of each month. We defined firm leverage as the ratio of book debt value (data51+data45) to the sum of book debt value and market capitalization. We also tried other firm characteristics besides those reported here: cash holdings, quick ratios, asset volatility, and distance-to-default. We found that the main conclusions drawn here do not change.

12

AMEX-NASDAQ value-weighted returns). An increase in either market volatility or market leverage, or a decrease in market returns, suggests a worsening economic outlook, which should be associated with an increase in credit risk. We define industry variables similarly—changes in industry volatility, changes in industry leverage, and changes in industry aggregate returns—and the same logic should hold at the industry level if there is an industry effect. We use the Fama-French 12-industry classification.[9]

Macroeconomic Variables

We use real GDP growth rate and changes in capacity utilization rate to describe the business cycle. [10] If credit risks are higher during an economic recession, we would see changes in CDS spreads negatively related to both real GDP growth rate and changes in capacity utilization rate. We also include inflation among our list of macroeconomic variables. Since previous studies have shown a negative relationship between real activity and inflation (see, e.g., Fama 1981, Geske and Roll 1983, Ram and Spencer 1983, and Stulz 1986), we expected a positive relationship between inflation and credit risk.

We use the following interest rate variables: changes in three-month T-bill rates, changes in term spreads (difference between the yields of 10-year T-bonds and three-month T-bills), and changes in credit spreads between BBB and AAA bonds and between AAA bonds and 10 year T-bonds. The relationship between the three-month T-bill rate and credit risk should be negative for two reasons. First, the Fed's monetary policy is pro-cyclical. Second, a higher interest rate can increase the risk-neutral drift of the

---

[9] Results using 48 industries are quite similar.

[10] We also tried some other macro variables, such as the industrial growth rate, changes in unemployment rate, and the Chicago Fed National Activity Index (CFNAI), and many others. We have not included these variables in the paper; they did not affect our results.

process of firm value, thus reducing credit risks (Longstaff and Schwartz 1995). Collin-Dufresne and colleagues (2001) and Duffee (1998) both documented a negative relationship between interest rate and credit risk. Credit risk should also be negatively related to the term spread (Estrella and Hardouvelis 1991, Estrella and Mishkin 1996, and Fama and French 1989) and positively related to both measures of credit spread (Chen 1991, Fama and French 1989, Friedman and Kuttner 1992, and Stock and Watson 1989).

Data Description

Table 1 provides summary statistics of the sample. For all firms, the mean CDS spread is 126.27 basis points (bps). The median and standard deviation suggest that the distribution of CDS spreads is quite skewed and volatile. The mean change in CDS spreads is small (–0.07 percent), but the range is wide (–17.78 to 23.43 percent). Both the high and low in CDS spread changes are found among the speculative-grade firms; these firms also have higher mean changes in CDS spreads. As expected, all three measures (CDS spreads, equity volatility, and firm leverage) are lower among investment-grade firms and higher among speculative-grade firms. Panel B of table 1 shows that the average CDS spread was highest in 2002; it declined sharply in 2003 and 2004, then leveled off.[11] The average monthly return on the NYSE-AMEX-NASDAQ index was 0.47 percent during the sample period, and the average annualized volatility was 19.08 percent. Over the entire sample period, the mean market leverage was 0.23. The average return across the industry portfolios was 0.57 percent, and the mean annualized industry volatility was 25.27 percent.

---

[11] The credit derivatives market was relatively immature in 2001, just crossing $1 trillion. By 2006, it was $34 trillion. So the prices observed in 2001 may not be the most efficient. To address this concern, we conducted the same analysis excluding observations from 2001 and reached similar conclusions.

Table 1. Descriptive Statistics

Table 1 shows the summary statistics of the variables used in the study. Panel A presents the descriptive statistics for the firm-level variables: five-year CDS spreads (in basis points), CDS spread percentage changes, equity returns, equity volatility, and leverage. The monthly equity volatility is computed as the annualized standard deviation based on daily returns. The firm leverage is computed as the ratio of book debt value to the sum of market capitalization and book debt value. The data are from January 2001 through December 2006. "Investment-grade" refers to firms with ratings at BAA or above; "speculative-grade" refers to firms with ratings below BAA. Panel B presents the descriptive statistics of CDS spreads by year. Panel C presents the summary statistics of the market and industry variables. VIX is the implied volatility of the S&P 500 index options obtained from the Chicago Board Options Exchange. The market return is the NYSE-AMEX-NASDAQ value-weighted index returns. Other market (industry) variables are the value-weighted average from all firms in the market (industry). We use the Fama-French 12-industry classification.

Panel A. Firm Characteristics

Variables	Mean	Median	Minimum	Maximum	Standard Deviation
All firms					
CDS (bps)	126.27	63.10	8.65	1,632.36	176.50
CDS change (%)	−0.07	−0.46	−17.78	23.43	2.52
Equity return (%)	1.23	1.13	−4.26	4.86	0.97
Equity volatility	0.31	0.28	0.13	0.78	0.11
Leverage	0.32	0.29	0.00	0.94	0.20
Investment-grade					
CDS (bps)	60.22	47.10	8.65	444.89	49.72
CDS change (%)	−0.42	−0.60	−5.06	7.93	1.77
Equity return (%)	1.18	1.13	−0.80	4.39	0.80
Equity volatility	0.27	0.25	0.16	0.64	0.07
Leverage	0.28	0.24	0.00	0.94	0.19
Speculative-grade					
CDS (bps)	295.23	223.24	53.81	1,632.36	255.05
CDS change (%)	8.26	5.78	−17.78	23.43	3.68
Equity return (%)	1.34	1.34	−4.26	4.86	1.30
Equity volatility	0.41	0.39	0.13	0.78	0.13
Leverage	0.44	0.43	0.06	0.92	0.19

Table 1. Descriptive Statistics (cont'd.)

Panel B. Summary Statistics of CDS Spreads (bps)

Year	Mean	Median	Minimum	Maximum	Standard Deviation
2001	151.67	83.33	17.83	3,249.57	284.40
2002	212.29	99.70	15.22	3,232.04	329.24
2003	150.72	69.62	9.84	2,508.39	219.41
2004	109.33	49.27	8.72	1,843.10	178.33
2005	107.17	44.90	5.21	2,181.16	200.90
2006	94.39	41.40	3.98	2,396.08	164.70

Panel C. Market- and Industry-Level Variables

Variables	Mean	Median	Minimum	Maximum	Standard Deviation
Market aggregate return (%)	0.47	1.11	−10.01	8.41	4.15
VIX (%)	19.08	16.69	10.91	39.69	6.98
Market leverage	0.23	0.23	0.19	0.27	0.01
Industry return (%)	0.57	1.57	−12.64	10.23	4.52
Industry volatility (%)	25.27	20.21	11.91	80.57	12.12
Industry leverage	0.23	0.17	0.07	0.48	0.15

Figure 1 plots the time-series variation in the seven macroeconomic variables used in this study. Real GDP growth was low and even entered negative territory at the beginning of the study period; it jumped in 2003 as the economy recovered. Similarly, capacity utilization shows a decline from 2001 to 2002, then a boost in 2003; it leveled off in 2005. The inflation rate is quite volatile during the study period.

The three-month T-bill rate shows a U-shape, depicting the Fed's policy to cut the interest rate during recessions and raise it during booms. The term spread has a humped shape: lower during the recession in early 2001 and higher as the recovery looms on the horizon. It declines sharply after mid-2004, as the Fed increased the short-term interest rate but the long-term interest rate did not change much. The spread between BBB and

Figure 1. Time Series of Macroeconomic Variables

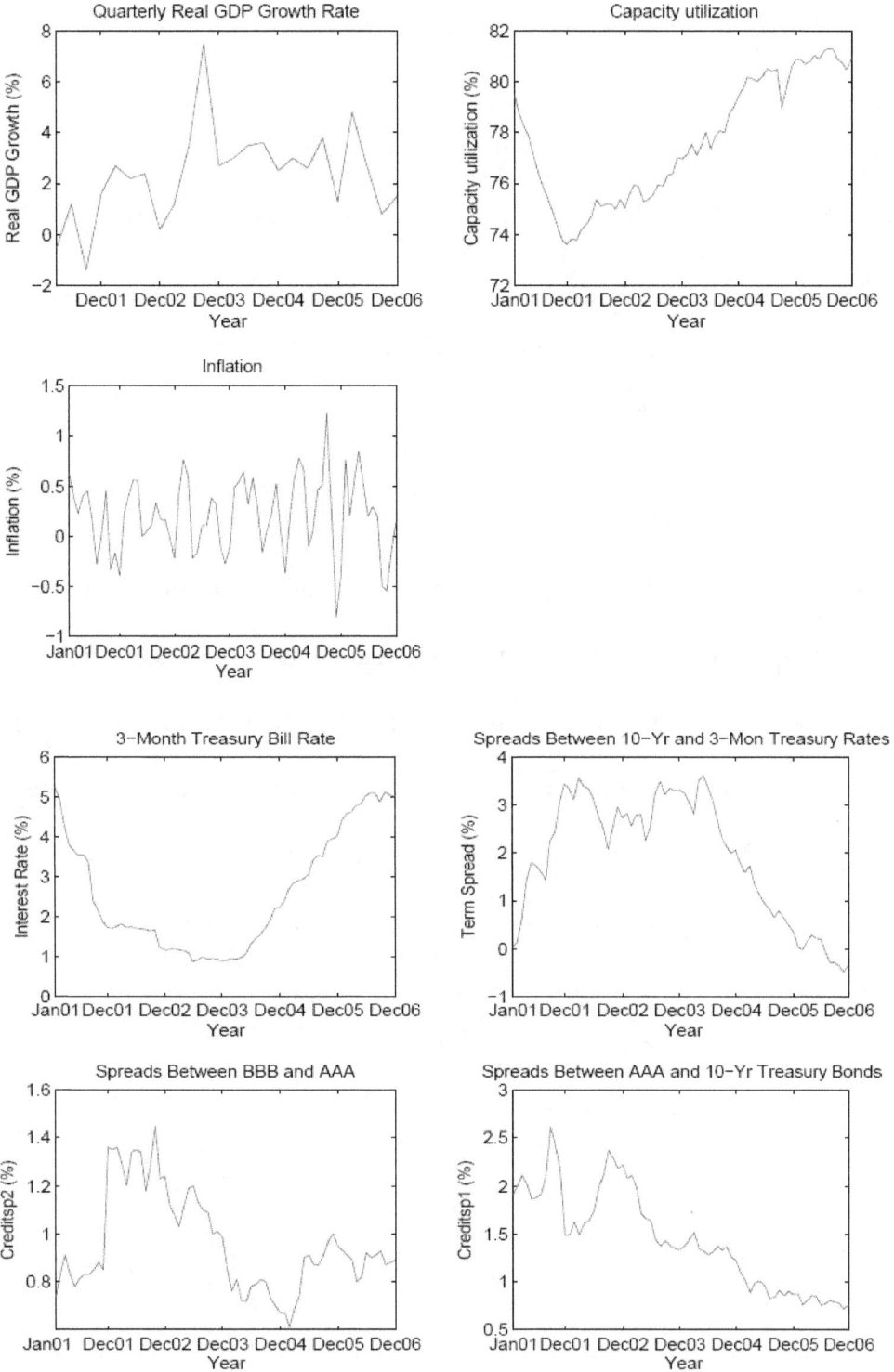

AAA yields shows a jump at the end of 2001 and then declines and reaches a low at the end of 2004. The spread between AAA and 10-year Treasury bonds shows a general decline over the sample period.

IV. Observable Risk Factors and Correlation in Credit Risk

Because most of our analyses involve panel data, our estimates are based on robust standard errors. We estimated these errors by assuming independence across firms, but we accounted for possible autocorrelation within the same firm. We use the contemporaneous variables on the right-hand-side variables.

Market and Macroeconomic Effect

Table 2 shows the effect of firm-level variables on changes in CDS spreads. We calculate the pairwise correlations (of the raw CDS spread changes or residuals from the regressions) and report the means in the last row of the table. The first column of table 2 shows that, without controlling for any observable covariates, the average correlation in changes in CDS spreads in the entire sample is 21 percent. The correlation ranges from a minimum of –30 percent to a maximum of 72 percent, and the interquartile spans a range of 30 percent.

Table 2. Effect of Firm Characteristics on the Correlation in Changes in CDS Spreads

Table 2 shows regression results of changes in CDS spread on firm-level variables: firm stock returns, changes in firm leverage, and changes in firm equity volatility. For each regression model, we report the average pairwise correlation in the residuals in the last row. The robust standard errors are in brackets. ** and *** represent statistical significance at the 5 percent and 1 percent levels, respectively.

Independent Variables	Model 1	Model 2	Model 3	Model 4	Model 5
Equity returns		–0.567***			–0.473***
		[0.023]			[0.025]
Change in firm leverage			1.662***		0.318***
			[0.114]		[0.084]
Chance in equity volatility				0.199***	0.148***
				[0.015]	[0.012]
Constant		0.003***	–0.002***	–0.003***	0.003***
		[0.001]	[0.001]	[0.001]	[0.001]
Observations	25,113	25,113	25,113	25,113	25,113
R^2		9%	5%	3%	11%
Correlation/residual correlation	0.21	0.17	0.14	0.16	0.13

Table 2 also shows that stock returns are negatively associated with changes in CDS spreads, while both volatility change and leverage change are positively related to CDS spread changes, consistent with expectations. The mean correlations reported in columns 2 through 5 are the residual correlations from each regression. It is clear that co-movements in all three firm-level variables among different firms can partially explain the correlation in the changes in CDS spreads. Among the three firm-level variables, changes in firm leverage can reduce the correlation most: from 21 percent to 14 percent. When all three variables are included, the correlation is reduced by 8 points to 13 percent.

Table 3 adds market-level variables to firm-level variables. Changes in market volatility are positively related to CDS spread changes. When used alone, change in market leverage is positively related to changes in CDS spreads. When combined with the other two market variables, the relationship between market leverage change and CDS spread change is significantly negative, suggesting the existence of multicollinearity. The aggregate market returns are negatively associated with changes in CDS spreads, regardless of whether they are used alone or in combination with other market variables. This evidence is consistent with our expectations but contrary to the findings of Duffie and colleagues (2007) and Lando and Nielsen (2008). Further, even with firm-level variables, market variables are still significantly associated with changes in CDS spreads, suggesting that the impact of market variables does not entirely channel through firm-level variables. This finding does not support the argument by Lando and Nielsen (2008).

However, even though market-level variables can explain changes in CDS spreads beyond what is explained by firm-level variables, they have only limited ability to reduce the correlation in credit risk across firms. The residual correlation decreases from 13 percent in column 5 of table 2 to 12 percent in column 4 of table 3.

Table 3. Effect of Market Variables on the Correlation in Changes in CDS Spreads

Table 3 shows regression results of changes in CDS spreads on firm-level and market-level variables. Firm-level variables are firm stock returns, changes in firm leverage, and changes in firm equity volatility. The market variables are changes in VIX, returns of the NYSE-AMEX-NASDAQ value-weighted index of the month, and changes in market leverage. For each regression model, we report the average pairwise correlation in the residuals in the last row. The robust standard errors are in brackets. ** and *** represent statistical significance at the 5 percent and 1 percent levels, respectively.

Independent Variables	Model 1	Model 2	Model 3	Model 4
Equity returns	–0.415***	–0.452***	–0.369***	–0.366***
	[0.025]	[0.025]	[0.026]	[0.026]
Change in firm leverage	0.325***	0.312***	0.326***	0.338***
	[0.084]	[0.084]	[0.084]	[0.084]
Change in equity volatility	0.137***	0.146***	0.136***	0.133***
	[0.012]	[0.012]	[0.012]	[0.012]
Change in VIX	0.006***			0.002***
	[0.000]			[0.001]
Change in market leverage		1.163***		–1.747***
		[0.198]		[0.248]
Market aggregate return			–0.632***	–0.720***
			[0.038]	[0.049]
Constant	0.003***	0.003***	0.007***	0.008***
	[0.001]	[0.001]	[0.001]	[0.001]
Observations	25,113	25,113	25,113	25,113
R^2	11%	11%	12%	12%
Residual correlation	0.14	0.13	0.12	0.12

In table 4, we add macroeconomic variables (instead of market-level variables) to firm-level variables to explain the changes in CDS spreads. Panel A shows that when they are used alone, both measures of business cycles are negatively associated with changes in CDS spreads, consistent with the expectation that credit risks are higher during a recession. We also find that CDS changes are negatively related to changes in three-month T-bill rates and changes in term spreads; and they are positively associated with inflation and both credit spread measures. These findings are consistent with expectations, confirming that macroeconomic factors affect a firm's credit risk. Among the macroeconomic variables, the two credit spreads show the greatest ability to account for correlation in changes in CDS spreads.

In panel B of table 4, we present four models. We include all the firm-level and macroeconomic variables in column 1. In column 2, we include the firm-level and two credit spread variables. In column 3, we include the firm-level and five macroeconomic variables (excluding credit spreads). In column 4, we include all the firm-level, market-level, and macroeconomic variables. Because of the correlations among them, some of the variables no longer have the right signs of regression coefficients and some other variables lose statistical significance. It is clear that a combination of all seven macroeconomic variables can reduce the correlation in changes in CDS spreads by 6 percentage points. Columns 2 and 3 show that the ability of macroeconomic variables to explain correlation in changes in CDS spread is largely due to the two credit spread measures. Column 4 of panel B shows that the market variables can contribute only marginal explanatory power beyond what is accounted for by the macroeconomic and firm-level variables.

Table 4. Effect of Macroeconomic Variables on the Correlation in Changes in CDS Spreads

Table 4 shows regression results of changes in CDS spreads on firm-level, market-level, and macroeconomic variables. Firm-level variables are firm stock returns, changes in firm leverage, and changes in firm equity volatility. The market variables are changes in VIX, returns of the NYSE-AMEX-NASDAQ value-weighted index of the month, and changes in market leverage. The macroeconomic variables are real GDP growth, changes in capacity utilization, inflation, changes in three-month T-bill rates, term spread (the difference between the 10-year T-bond yield and the three-month T-bill yield), the yield difference between BBB and AAA bonds, and the yield difference between AAA bonds and 10-year T-bonds. For each regression model, we report the average pairwise correlation in the residuals in the last row. In panel A, we include each macroeconomic variable in the regression models one by one. In panel B, we use combinations of macroeconomic and market variables. The robust standard errors are in brackets. ** and *** represent statistical significance at the 5 percent and 1 percent levels, respectively.

Panel A

Independent Variables	Model 1	Model 2	Model 3	Model 4	Model 5	Model 6	Model 7
Equity returns	−0.470*** [0.025]	−0.475*** [0.025]	−0.462*** [0.025]	−0.465*** [0.025]	−0.466*** [0.025]	−0.458*** [0.025]	−0.424*** [0.025]
Change in firm leverage	0.306*** [0.084]	0.317*** [0.084]	0.324*** [0.085]	0.318*** [0.084]	0.319*** [0.084]	0.321*** [0.084]	0.311*** [0.083]
Change in equity volatility	0.149*** [0.012]	0.149*** [0.012]	0.142*** [0.012]	0.150*** [0.012]	0.150*** [0.012]	0.144*** [0.012]	0.133*** [0.012]
Real GDP growth	−0.479*** [0.053]						
Change in capacity utilization		−0.018*** [0.002]					
Inflation			2.208*** [0.234]				
Change in term spread				−3.129*** [0.388]			
Change in nominal interest rate					−5.769*** [0.532]		
Change in spread between BBB and AAA						28.951*** [1.428]	
Change in spread between AAA and T-bond							19.069*** [1.026]
Constant	0.015*** [0.002]	0.004*** [0.001]	−0.002** [0.001]	0.001 [0.001]	0.005*** [0.001]	0.003*** [0.001]	0.006*** [0.001]
Observations	25,113	25,113	25,113	25,113	25,113	25,113	25,113
R^2	11%	11%	11%	11%	11%	12%	12%
Residual correlation	0.13	0.13	0.13	0.13	0.13	0.10	0.12

Table 4. Effect of Macroeconomic Variables on the Correlation in Changes in CDS Spreads (cont'd.)

Panel B

Independent Variables	Model 1	Model 2	Model 3	Model 4
Firm returns	−0.370*** [0.025]	−0.390*** [0.025]	−0.423*** [0.025]	−0.359*** [0.026]
Change in firm leverage	0.323*** [0.083]	0.314*** [0.083]	0.323*** [0.083]	0.328*** [0.083]
Change in firm volatility	0.116*** [0.011]	0.123*** [0.011]	0.145*** [0.012]	0.114*** [0.011]
Real GDP growth	−0.232*** [0.063]		−0.365*** [0.062]	−0.251*** [0.064]
Change in capacity utilization	0.015*** [0.002]		−0.001 [0.002]	0.014*** [0.003]
Inflation	3.813*** [0.293]		3.840*** [0.278]	3.569*** [0.296]
Change in term spread	−0.06 [0.536]		−6.858*** [0.442]	0.005 [0.526]
Change in three-month T-bill rate	−4.564*** [0.796]		−10.710*** [0.742]	−4.263*** [0.798]
Change in spread between BBB and AAA	40.620*** [1.558]	36.916*** [1.400]		39.106*** [1.622]
Change in spread between AAA and T-bond	21.627*** [1.267]	24.907*** [1.014]		20.344*** [1.243]
Change in VIX				0.002** [0.001]
Change in market leverage				−0.640** [0.251]
Market aggregate return				−0.08 [0.050]
Constant	0.005*** [0.002]	0.007*** [0.001]	0.006*** [0.002]	0.007*** [0.002]
Observations	25,113	25,113	25,113	25,113
R^2	16%	15%	12%	16%
Residual correlation	0.07	0.08	0.12	0.07

Industry Effect

Table 5 shows the average pairwise correlation in CDS spread changes among firms in each of the 11 Fama-French industries.[12] The table shows much variation in correlation in credit risk among firms in the same industry. Over the study period, the energy sector has the highest correlation among all industries, whereas the health care sector has the lowest correlation. Only four of the 11 industries have a higher average correlation than the overall average of 21 percent.

The ranking of correlation by industry changed over the six-year study period. The financial industry had the highest correlation in 2001 and 2002, suggesting that an economic downturn affects financial firms more than others. The energy industry had the highest correlation from 2004 to 2006, likely driven by volatile price movements in oil. The health care, medical equipment, and drug industries had the lowest correlations in three of the six years, and consumer nondurable goods had the lowest correlation in two years. These findings suggest that less cyclical industries have lower correlations in credit risk.

Table 5 shows the existence of an industry effect, which we examine in table 6. Panel A of table 6 shows firm-level and industry-level variables. We find that changes in industry volatility are positively related to changes in CDS spreads, whereas industry returns are negatively related to changes in CDS spreads. When it is used alone, industry leverage change is positively related to changes in CDS spreads. When all three industry variables are used together, industry return and volatility retain their signs of regression

---

[12] We omitted the 12th industry (which consisted of miscellaneous firms) from the analysis.

Table 5. Correlation in CDS Spread Changes Across Industries

Table 5 shows the average pairwise correlation in CDS spread changes across the 11 industries in our sample. We use the Fama-French 12-industry classification. Ind1 refers to consumer nondurables; Ind2 to consumer durables; Ind3 to manufacturing; Ind4 to energy; Ind5 to chemicals and allied products; Ind6 to business equipment; Ind7 to telephone and television transmission; Ind8 to utilities; Ind9 to wholesale, retail, and other services; Ind10 to health care, medical equipment, and drugs; and Ind11 to finance. The classification follows the rules set by the French data library. We omitted the Industry 12 category, which includes mines, construction, building materials, transportation, hotels, business services, and entertainment. We required a minimum of six observations to calculate pairwise correlations; there were not enough observations for Ind10 in 2001 to make this calculation.

Year	Ind1	Ind2	Ind3	Ind4	Ind5	Ind6	Ind7	Ind8	Ind9	Ind10	Ind11
2001	0.12	0.44	0.44	0.63	0.24	0.36	0.51	0.28	0.41	—	0.65
2002	0.13	0.43	0.26	0.26	0.14	0.41	0.43	0.38	0.24	0.17	0.45
2003	0.20	0.33	0.15	0.24	0.05	0.13	0.25	0.36	0.17	0.03	0.29
2004	0.24	0.26	0.21	0.35	0.17	0.21	0.26	0.32	0.23	0.14	0.30
2005	0.22	0.28	0.23	0.55	0.18	0.22	0.22	0.35	0.20	0.23	0.31
2006	0.06	0.07	0.09	0.33	0.17	0.11	0.12	0.26	0.22	0.06	0.13
2001–2006	0.16	0.28	0.18	0.35	0.18	0.17	0.16	0.29	0.19	0.11	0.22

Table 6. Effect of Industry-Level Variables on the Correlation in CDS Spread Changes

Table 6 shows regression results of changes in CDS spreads on firm-level, industry-level, market-level, and macroeconomic variables. Firm-level variables are firm stock returns, changes in firm leverage, and changes in firm equity volatility. Industry-level variables are based on the Fama-French 12-industry classification: monthly returns of the value-weighted industry portfolio, changes in industry equity volatility, and changes in industry leverage. Market-level variables are changes in VIX, returns of the NYSE-AMEX-NASDAQ value-weighted index of the month, and changes in market leverage. Macroeconomic variables are real GDP growth, changes in capacity utilization, inflation, changes in the three-month T-bill rate, term spread (the difference between the 10-year T-bond yield and the three-month T-bill yield), yield difference between BBB and AAA bonds, and yield difference between AAA bonds and the 10-year T-bond. For each regression model, we show the average pairwise correlation in the residuals in the last row. In panel A, we include each industry variable in the regression model one by one. In panel B, we use combinations of the firm-level, industry-level, market-level, and macroeconomic variables. The robust standard errors are in brackets. ** and *** represent statistical significance at the 5 percent and 1 percent levels, respectively.

Panel A

Independent Variables	Model 1	Model 2	Model 3	Model 4
Equity returns	−0.368***	−0.452***	−0.468***	−0.368***
	[0.028]	[0.025]	[0.026]	[0.027]
Change in firm leverage	0.323***	0.308***	0.314***	0.325***
	[0.084]	[0.084]	[0.085]	[0.084]
Change in equity volatility	0.138***	0.102***	0.147***	0.106***
	[0.012]	[0.012]	[0.012]	[0.012]
Industry returns	−0.425***			−0.418***
	[0.034]			[0.036]
Change in industry volatility		0.219***		0.161***
		[0.025]		[0.026]
Change in industry leverage			0.174	−0.423***
			[0.098]	[0.095]
Constant	0.005***	0.003***	0.003***	0.005***
	[0.001]	[0.001]	[0.001]	[0.001]
Observations	25,113	25,113	25,113	25,113
R^2	11%	11%	11%	12%
Residual correlation	0.12	0.13	0.13	0.12

Table 6. Effect of Industry-Level Variables on the Correlation in CDS Spread Changes (cont'd.)

Panel B

Independent Variables	Model 1	Model 2	Model 3	Model 4
Firm returns	−0.352*** [0.027]	−0.355*** [0.027]	−0.351*** [0.027]	
Change in firm leverage	0.329*** [0.083]	0.337*** [0.084]	0.332*** [0.083]	
Change in firm volatility	0.106*** [0.012]	0.107*** [0.012]	0.106*** [0.012]	
Industry returns	−0.116*** [0.036]	−0.109** [0.043]	−0.098** [0.042]	−0.427*** [0.042]
Change in industry volatility	0.048* [0.027]	0.132*** [0.026]	0.042 [0.027]	0.280*** [0.026]
Change in industry leverage	−0.331*** [0.090]	−0.314*** [0.091]	−0.306*** [0.090]	−0.266*** [0.095]
Change in VIX		0.001** [0.001]	0.001** [0.001]	0.001** [0.001]
Change in market leverage		−1.468*** [0.245]	−0.469* [0.249]	−1.643*** [0.252]
Market aggregate return		−0.610*** [0.056]	−0.012 [0.057]	−0.514*** [0.059]
Real GDP growth	−0.218*** [0.064]		−0.246*** [0.065]	−0.309*** [0.069]
Change in capacity utilization	0.014*** [0.002]		0.014*** [0.003]	−0.004* [0.003]
Inflation	3.575*** [0.301]		3.509*** [0.302]	2.457*** [0.285]
Change in term spread	−0.270 [0.539]		−0.229 [0.534]	−5.282*** [0.441]
Change in three-month T-bill rate	−4.648*** [0.830]		−4.530*** [0.833]	−8.039*** [0.743]
Change in spread between BBB and AAA bonds	20.020*** [1.230]		19.615*** [1.222]	
Change in spread between AAA bonds and T-bond	38.990*** [1.626]		38.468*** [1.648]	
Constant	0.006*** [0.002]	0.008*** [0.001]	0.007*** [0.002]	0.010*** [0.002]
Observations	25,113	25,113	25,113	25,387
R^2	16%	12%	16%	9%
Residual correlation	0.07	0.13	0.07	0.12

coefficients, while industry leverage shows an opposite sign, suggesting the existence of multicollinearity. In the first three columns of panel B, we add market and macroeconomic variables and find that results on the industry-level variables generally do not change.

The last rows of table 6 show that the industry effect has only a trivial effect on the correlation in CDS spread changes. When all observable variables are included (column 3, panel B), the average correlation is 7 percent; in column 4, panel B of table 4—where industry variables are not included—the correlation is also 7 percent. This suggests that although industry variables are significantly related to changes in CDS spreads, the industry effect only marginally accounts for correlation in credit risk across firms.

Contribution by Contagion

We have shown that common risk factors such as market variables, industry variables, and macroeconomic variables (excluding credit spreads) have a limited effect on correlation in changes in CDS spreads, and that the correlation is mainly driven by firm-level variables and credit spreads. However, both common risk factors and contagion can affect firm-level variables and credit spreads. To assess the upper bound of the correlations that could be attributed to contagion, we include in the last column of panel B in table 6 the variables affected only by common risk factors. We find that the average residual correlation is 0.12.

Comparing column 3 in panel B of table 6 with the first column in table 2, where no control variables are included, we conclude that the observable covariates can explain 14 percentage points of the correlations in credit risks. The remaining 7 percentage points should be due to contagion; thus, contagion contributes to at least one-third of the correlations in changes in CDS spreads. Further, comparing the last column in panel B of table 6 with the first column in table 2, we conclude that the contagion-free common risk factors can explain at least 9 percentage points, with the remaining 12 percentage points possibly caused by contagion. Thus, contagion could account for as much as 57 percent of the overall correlation in credit risks.

These numbers are much higher than those reported by Das and colleagues (2007) and suggest that contagion is not only statistically significant but also economically significant in causing correlation in credit risk. Our evidence suggests that future research in credit modeling must take contagion into consideration.

Additional Investigations

Our findings were derived from linear models. Can nonlinear terms be responsible for the correlation in credit risk? To address this concern, we included higher order terms and some interactive terms in the model, and found that the results did not change qualitatively. For example, when we included both the first- and second-order terms of all the observable variables, the average residual correlation declined to 6.2 percent, which is still statistically and economically significant. Thus, adding nonlinear interactive terms does not shrink the residual correlation drastically. The same was true when we added third- and fourth-order terms. Although it is possible that a particular combination of higher order and interactive terms may lead to close-to-zero residual correlations, we are wary of this approach because reduced-form models are very atheoretical and additional higher order terms lack theoretical reasoning, risking overfitting and poor out-of-sample fit.

Is contagion the result of illiquidity in the market? To address this question, we included several liquidity measures in the regression model, such as a stock market liquidity measure proposed by Amihud (2002) and a measure describing the CDS market depth (the number of contributors for the CDS spread quotes). Even after taking market liquidity into consideration, the residual correlation did not shrink substantially and was still significantly positive. The finding suggests that market illiquidity may not be the sole contributor to contagion.

We also investigated whether contagion shows up only during economic downturns. In each year of our study period, the proportion of correlation in credit risk that could not be explained by the observable factors exceeded 30 percent. Therefore, it seems that contagion is a general phenomenon in various economic conditions. Because of the magnitude, it is important for future research to incorporate unobservable risk factors into credit models, both theoretically and empirically.

V. Correlations in Changes in CDS Spreads Over Time and by Rating Group

The second question we investigated is how the correlation pattern changes over time and across different credit quality firms. We grouped firms according to their credit ratings; panel A of table 7 shows the average correlation in CDS spread changes over time among investment-grade firms and speculative-grade firms.

The first column shows variation in credit risk correlation over time. The mean correlation is the highest at 0.34 in 2001, when the economy was in recession. As the economic environment improved from 2001 to 2003, the mean correlation in CDS spread changes declined from 0.34 to 0.23 in 2002 and to 0.14 in 2003. This pattern is consistent with the theoretical prediction that the correlation should be higher during economic downturns (see, e.g., Erlenmaier and Gersbach 2001, and Gersbach and Lipponer 2000). The increased correlation in 2004 and 2005 is possibly due to credit problems at General Motors and Ford Motor Company. A study by Acharya, Schaefer, and Zhang (2008) shows that the increase in credit risk in these two companies led to excess co-movement in CDS spreads of all firms. These authors found that the co-movement quickly declined after the two companies were downgraded, which is consistent with the low correlation in 2006.

Table 7. Pairwise Correlation Over Time and by Rating Groups

Table 7 shows the average pairwise correlation of all firms and by rating groups. Firms rated BAA and above are classified as investment-grade; firms rated BA and below are classified as speculative-grade. Panel A shows average pairwise correlations in the changes in CDS spreads; panel B shows average pairwise correlations in the changes in asset volatility.

Panel A. Changes in CDS Spreads			
Year	All Firms	Investment-Grade	Speculative-Grade
2001	0.34	0.34	0.35
2002	0.23	0.22	0.29
2003	0.14	0.14	0.21
2004	0.20	0.21	0.28
2005	0.22	0.21	0.29
2006	0.12	0.13	0.13
2001–2006	0.21	0.21	0.23
Panel B. Changes in Asset Volatility			
Year	All Firms	Investment-Grade	Speculative-Grade
2001	0.20	0.28	0.11
2002	0.28	0.36	0.20
42003	0.37	0.45	0.28
2004	0.05	0.08	0.01
2005	0.07	0.09	0.04
2006	0.12	0.13	0.09
2001–2006	0.15	0.17	0.08

Columns 2 and 3 in table 7 show that the variation in correlation over time follows the same pattern for both investment-grade and speculative-grade firms. Both groups experienced the highest correlation in 2001, a decline from 2001 to 2003, an increase in 2004 and 2005, and the lowest correlation in 2006. These findings are inconsistent with those of Das and colleagues (2006): although these authors document some degree of variation in the default risk correlation, the variation does not correspond to the business cycle.

Panel A of table 7 suggests that the correlation in credit risk is higher among speculative-grade firms than among investment-grade firms. Over the study period, the average correlation in CDS spread changes was 0.23 among firms with high credit ratings and 0.21 among firms with low credit ratings. For each year of the study period, the correlation in the changes in CDS spreads was higher among firms with low credit ratings than among those with high credit ratings, and this correlation is highest among firms with low ratings during the economic downturn in 2001. These results are consistent with theoretical predictions (see, e.g., Erlenmaier and Gersbach 2001, and Zhou 2001). The results are not consistent with those reported by Das and colleagues (2006) and Lopez (2002), who show that the correlation is higher among firms with high credit ratings.

The results in Das and colleagues (2006) and Lopez (2002) are derived from the estimated default probability using the Merton model. To reconcile our findings with the findings in these studies, we resorted to the Merton model and backed out monthly distance-to-default, asset value, and asset volatility. Das and colleagues (2006) say that the correlation in default intensity is driven by the correlation in asset volatility, so in panel B of table 7 we report the correlation in asset volatility by year and by ratings. This panel shows that the correlation in asset volatility is indeed higher among firms with high credit ratings than among those with low credit ratings. Over the study period, the average correlation in asset volatility was 0.17 among the former and 0.08 among the latter. The correlation in asset volatility was lowest (0.20) in 2001, when the economy entered the recession, and highest (0.37) in 2003, when it had fully recovered. Columns 2 and 3 of this panel show that the highest average correlation in asset volatility (0.45) was in 2003 among investment-grade firms, while the lowest (0.01) was in 2004 among firms with low credit ratings. These counterintuitive patterns are consistent with those documented by Das and colleagues (2006) and Lopez (2002).

We believe that the patterns shown in panel B of table 7 may be driven by the oversimplified assumptions behind the Merton model. Some researchers have documented that the Merton model cannot predict default events well (see, e.g., Bharath and Shumway 2007, Jones et al. 1984, and Zhou 2001). We believe that correlation patterns based on the Merton model may not be the most reliable.

VI. Conclusions

In this paper, we examine the correlation in credit risk using CDS data. We find that observable variables at the firm, industry, and market levels, as well as macroeconomic variables, cannot fully explain the correlation in credit risk, leaving at least one-third of the correlation in credit risk unaccounted for during the study period (2001–2006). These findings suggest that contagion may be a common phenomenon in an economy and that the doubly stochastic assumption may not hold in general. Because of the large proportion of correlation that cannot be explained by observable risk factors, future research in credit modeling should focus on incorporating unobservable risk factors into models.

We also find that credit risk correlation is higher during economic downturns and higher among firms with low credit ratings than among those with high credit ratings. These findings are consistent with the theoretical predictions but inconsistent with some empirical findings based on the Merton default probability measure. We contend that our results are more reliable because of the oversimplified assumptions behind Merton's model and the evidence in the literature that the Merton default probability measure cannot accurately forecast default probabilities.

References

Acharya, V., S. Schaefer, and Y. L. Zhang. 2008. *Liquidity Risk and Correlation Risk: A Clinical Study of the General Motors and Ford Downgrade of May 2005.* Working paper, London Business School.

Amihud, Yakov. 2002. Illiquidity and Stock Returns: Cross-Section and Time-Series Effects. *Journal of Financial Markets*, 5, 31–56.

Anderson, R. W., S. Sundaresan, and P. Tychon. 1996. Strategic Analysis of Contingent Claims. *European Economic Review*, 40, 871–881.

Bergman, Y., and J. Callen. 1991. Opportunistic Underinvestment in Debt Renegotiation and Capital Structure. *Journal of Financial Economics*, 29, 137–171.

Bharath, S., and Taylor Shumway. 2007. Forecasting Default With the Merton Distance-to-Default Model. *Review of Financial Studies*, forthcoming.

Carling, Kenneth, Tor Jacobson, Jesper Linde, and Kasper Roszbach. 2007. Corporate Credit Risk Modeling and the Macroeconomy. *Journal of Banking and Finance*, 31, 845–868.

Chen, N. 1991. Financial Investment Opportunities and the Macroeconomy. *Journal of Finance*, 46, 529–554.

Collin-Dufresne, P., R. Goldstein, and J. S. Martin. 2001. The Determinants of Credit Spread Changes. *Journal of Finance*, 56(6), 2177–2207.

Couderc, Fabien, and Olivier Renault. 2005. *Times-to-Default: Life Cycle, Global, and Industry Cycle Impact.* FAME Research Paper Series.

Das, S., D. Duffie, N. Kapadia, and L. Saita. 2007. Common Failings: How Corporate Defaults Are Correlated. *Journal of Finance*, 62, 93–117.

Das, S., L. Freed, G. Geng, and N. Kapadia. 2006. Correlated Default Risk. *Journal of Fixed Income*, 16, 7–32.

Duffee, Gregory R. 1998. The Relation Between Treasury Yields and Corporate Bond Yield Spreads. *Journal of Finance*, 53, 2225–2241.

Duffie, D., A. Eckner, G. Horel, and L. Saita. 2008. Frailty Correlated Default. *Journal of Finance*, forthcoming.

Duffie, D., and K. J. Singleton. 1999. Modeling the Term Structure of Defaultable Bonds. *Review of Financial Studies*, 12, 687–720.

Duffie, D., L. Saita, and K. Wang. 2007. Multi-Period Corporate Failure Prediction With Stochastic Covariates. *Journal of Financial Economics*, 83, 635–665.

Erlenmaier, U., and H. Gersbach. 2001. *Default Probabilities and Default Correlations,* Working paper, University of Heidelberg.

Estrella, A., and G. A. Hardouvelis. 1991. The Term Structure As a Predictor of Real Economic Activity. *Journal of Finance*, 46, 555–576.

Estrella, A., and F. S. Mishkin. 1996. The Yield Curve As a Predicator of U.S. Recessions. *Federal Reserve Bank of New York: Current Issues in Economics and Finance*, 2, 1–6.

Fama, E. 1981. Stock Returns, Real Activity, Inflation, and Money. *American Economic Review*, 71, 545–565.

Fama, E. F., and K. R. French. 1989. Business Conditions and Expected Returns on Stocks and Bonds. *Journal of Financial Economics*, 25, 23–49.

Figlewski, S., H. Frydman, and W. Liang. 2006. *Modeling the Effect of Macroeconomic Factors on Corporate Default and Credit Rating Transitions*. Working paper, New York University.

Frank, J., and W. Torous. 1989. An Empirical Investigation of Firms in Reorganization. *Journal of Finance*, 44, 747–779.

Frank, J., and W. Torous. 1994. A Comparison of Financial Recontracting in Workouts and Chapter 11 Reorganizations. *Journal of Financial Economics*, 35, 349–370.

Friedman, B. M., and K. N. Kuttner. 1992. Money, Income, Prices, and Interest Rates. *American Economic Review*, 82, 472–492.

Gersbach, Hans, and Alexander Lipponer. 2000. *The Correlation Effect*. Athens: European Financial Management Association.

Gertner, R., and D. Scharfstein. 1991. A Theory of Workouts and the Effects of Reorganization Law. *Journal of Finance*, 46, 1189–1222.

Geske, R., and R. Roll. 1983. "The Monetary and Fiscal Linkage Between Stock Returns and Inflation. *Journal of Finance*, 38: 1–33.

Giesecke, Kay. 2004. Correlated Default With Incomplete Information. *Journal of Banking and Finance*, 28, 1521–1545.

Gupton, Greg M., David T. Hamilton, and Alexander Berthault. 2001. *Default and Recovery Rates of Corporate Bond Issuers: 2000.* New York: Moody's Investor Service.

Hull, John, and Alan White. 2001. Valuing Credit Default Swaps II: Modeling Default Correlations. *Journal of Derivatives*, 8, 12–22.

Hull, John, Mirela Predescu, and Alan White. 2004. The Relation Between Credit Default Swap Spreads, Bond Yields, and Credit Rating Announcements. *Journal of Banking and Finance*, 28, 2789–2811.

Jarrow, R. A., D. Lando, and S. Turnbull. 1995. Pricing Derivatives on Financial Securities Subject to Default Risk.. *Journal of Finance*, 50, 53–86.

Jarrow, R. A., and F. Yu. 2001. Counterparty Risk and the Pricing of Defaultable Securities. *Journal of Finance*, 56, 1765–1799.

Jones, P., S. Mason, and E. Rosenfeld. 1984. Contingent Claims Analysis of Corporate Capital Structures: An Empirical Analysis. *Journal of Finance*, 39, 611–625.

Jorion, P., and Zhang, G. Y. 2007. Good and Bad Credit Contagion: Evidence From Credit Default Swaps. *Journal of Financial Economics*, 84(3), 860–883.

Lando, D. 1998. On Cox Processes and Credit Risky Securities. *Review of Derivatives Research*, 2, 99–120.

Lando, D., and M. S. Nielsen. 2008. *Correlation in Corporate Defaults: Contagion or Conditional Independence?* Working paper, Mannheim University.

Longstaff, Francis A., and Eduardo Schwartz. 1995. A Simple Approach to Valuing Risky Fixed and Floating Rate Debt. *Journal of Finance*, 50, 789–821.

Lopez, J. 2002. The Empirical Relationship Between Average Asset Correlation, Firm Probability of Default, and Asset Size. *Working Papers in Applied Economic Theory 2002-05.* Federal Reserve Bank of San Francisco.

Merton, Robert. 1974. On the Pricing of Corporate Debt: The Risk Structure of Interest Rates. *Journal of Finance*, 29, 449–470.

Ram, R., and D. E. Spencer. 1983. Stock Returns, Real Activity, Inflation and Money: Comment. *American Economic Review*, 73, 463–470.

Schönbucher, Philipp, and Dirk Schubert. 2001. *Copula Dependent Default Risk in Intensity Models.* Working paper, Bonn University.

Stock, J., and M. W. Watson. 1989. New Indexes of Coincident and Leading Indicators. *NBER Macroeconomics*, 4, 351–394.

Stulz, R. M. 1986. Asset Pricing and Expected Inflation. *Journal of Finance*, 41, 209–223.

Zhou, C. 2001. An Analysis of Default Correlations and Multiple Defaults. *Review of Financial Studies*, 14, 555–576.